This book belongs to an dog called:

Everyone should experience the
love of a dog in their life.
It is pure, simple and uncomplicated.

Table of Contents

How to Use This Book

Throughout the pages of this book you will find much of the information you need to be a successful and happy pet owner. There are plenty of important points along with tips and tricks for planning ahead, toilet training and socialization (to mention just a few). If you stick to the guidelines and follow the suggestions outlined you will have many happy years with your pet.

With our busy lives there is much to remember and keep track of in order to take the best care of your pooch and get the most from your time together. The goal of this book is to help you along the way and make things a little easier.

Inside you will find record sheets and trackers where you can enter all the key information so you don't have remember everything. This frees up your brain so you can truly enjoy the time you spend with your dog. To really get the most benefit you should keep the trackers up to date. Take a few minutes a day to reflect and jot down any important information.

Because we humans adore our pets we have also included plenty of space to record our happy memories and the milestones in your dogs life!

Dogs are not our whole life, but they make our lives whole.

Enjoy !

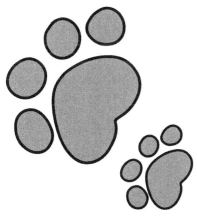  

About Me

Breed: _____   Birthday: _____

Coat color: _____   Eye color: _____

Gender: _____

Special Markings: _____

ID chip #: _____

Address: _____

_____

_____

Phone number: _____

_____

Planning with the Household

- Find a vet close by where you have easy access and parking. Get some recommendations from friends. Register and get an appointment in your calendar for a check-up and vaccinations.

- Think about pet insurance. This can help a lot with vet bills in the event that your pooch takes ill. It can also protect you if your dog does any damage to someone else or their property.

- Agree the common words you will all use with your dog for the initial simple commands things like heel, sit, stay, No. Also agree common words for walk, No/ Stop.

- Agree house rules – are there any areas of the house off limits for your puppy? Set your boundaries.

- You will have to change some habits for a while like leaving food on the counter or putting grocery bags on the floor.

- Get into the habit of picking up after yourself, do not leave shoes, bags etc. lying around, as these look like great chew toys to your new pup!

- Think about the daily routine for the household. Will you need to arrange someone to come in to walk or look after the dog? Will you need a doggy day care? Remember dogs and especially puppies do not do well left on their own for more than a few hours.

- Consider registering for puppy training or socialization classes. Great way for you to meet other puppy owners too and share some tips. They are also highly entertaining!

Preparing - at the Shops

- Crate. Using a crate helps a lot to speed up the house training time and provides a safe area for your puppy if you need to leave the house for a while.

- Soft cosy washable bed / bedding.

- Food and water bowls. Remember to have a decent size water bowl in particular so when leave the house there will be plenty available.

- Food and maybe some treats for training—talk to your vet about an appropriate diet. Consider low fat treats especially when you are training as they may end up putting on some weight.

- Collar and leash. Your local pet store will help you here. Remember you will need a few as you puppy grows so no need to go for the top end. Go for one that is easy to put on.

- Toys, especially chew toys to keep them busy. Make sure they are suitable for puppies.

- Stain and odor removing cleaners. Believe me you will need these for the first few weeks.

- Consider baby or dog gates to block off sections of your house.

- Newspaper or puppy pads for house training.

- Brushes and grooming tools. You don't have to go high end expensive here. Sometimes the simplest products are the best.

- Poo bags to pick the parcels that your new little four legged bundle will leave for you.

Fast Facts About Golden Retrievers

- Golden Retrievers are one of the top 3 most popular dogs
  This is mostly due to their sociable nature, love of people, loyalty and trainability.

- Goldens make great family dogs. Golden Retrievers are very pack oriented. They simply love hanging out with the people who make up their "family" or pack.

- They are excellent hunting companions.
  Golden Retrievers were first developed to retrieve fowl for hunters at the Scottish estate of Sir Dudley Majoribanks.

- Goldies are simply gorgeous!
  Combine a statuesque build with a lustrous coat in all shades of gold, a well-groomed Golden is a sight to behold.

- They are natural athletes.
  Goldens love to chase and catch—and they are very good at it. But all this athleticism means Golden Retrievers need exercise - lots!

- They have a long life span.
  With a life span of 12-14 years, Goldens are companions that will be around for you to enjoy for a long time. Thanks!

- They are easy to train.
  So easy, in fact, that they are a popular choice for movies and TV shows. They are very food oriented – they will do anything for it!

- They make great therapy and service dogs.
  Partly because they are so highly trainable, Golden Retrievers are excellent choices for therapy or canine assistance.

- Golden Retrievers are known to become sad and even depressed when left alone for long periods of time.

My Humans

People in my family:

_____

_____

_____

_____

_____

My Favorite: _____

_____

Spoils me the most: _____

_____

_____

Ways I am spoiled: _____

_____

_____

My First Day

Where I came from:
_____
_____

Journey Home:
_____
_____
_____

People I met: _____
_____

First reactions: _____
_____

Other Memories:
_____
_____
_____

My first Photo

 # Tips for New Puppy Owners

- Allow lots of time
  Training your puppy is going to take some time and effort.
  You will need to be patient. The more time and focus you
  give this in the early weeks, the sooner you will have a well
  behaved, trained puppy that everyone will adore.

- Encourage curiosity and independence, not fear.
  Puppies can be nervous of new things and situations. If
  they cry, try not to always reassure them.

- Encourage new things
  After their vaccinations, get out there with your puppy to
  discover new things. Go for plenty of walks together -this
  helps your dog to fa iliari e themselves with busy places,
  crowds of people, traffic noise, children and other animals
  too. It is good to take a new puppy out for trips in in the
  car too and invite plenty of visitors to your house. Check to
  see if there are any puppy socialization classes in your
  nei hborhood. These classes can be great fun for all!

- Build your puppy's independence
  You should gradually increase the amount of time you leave
  your puppy alone to build their independence. e know it's
  hard, but try to ignore crying. They will be fine and get used
  to it in no time.

- No teeth please!
  Biting play is normal between littermates and other puppies, but biting play with humans is definitely not something you want to encourage. Every time their teeth touch
  a humans skin, stop with an abrupt "No!" and with-draw all
  attention.

Puppy Proofing Tips

- You'll need to puppy-proof the area where your youngster will spend most of his time the first few months. You should think about doing the following:

  ○ Taping loose electrical cords to baseboards or put them out of reach. A puppy's teeth will sink right through. As well as potential danger to your pooch, repairs and replacements can be costly.

  ○ Storing household chemicals on high shelves.

  ○ Removing plants, rugs, and breakables.

  ○ Removing anything hanging within reach of you puppy like curtains, blinds. This may only be temporary while your puppy is learning the ropes!

  ○ Making space and setting up your crate ahead of time and install gates if necessary.

  ○ Once you think you've completely puppy-proofed, lie on the floor and look around once more to get a puppy's-eye view.

- For things that can't move like furniture legs, skirting or base boards you could consider an anti-chew spray. Your pet shop or vet are likley to stock one. You could make your own spray with chili and water which does the trick nicely. How ever, some dogs dont mind the taste and will keep chewing regardless.

Vet Details

Name: _____

Address: _____

Phone number: _____

Opening Hours: _____

_____

My first visit to the vet was for:

_____

_____

People I met: _____

I liked ☐   disliked it ☐

_____

Vaccination Records

Vaccination	Date	Age	Note

_____

_____

_____

_____

_____

_____

Crate Training Tips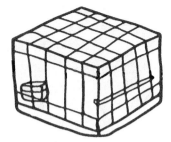

- In your puppy's mind, his crate should be his "safe place" to go!

- Using positive encouragement and teaching your puppy that his crate is a good place to be, will help him to be a more relaxed and happy puppy. You can encourage him in with his favorite treats and toys. You should keep his favorites for his crate, so he feels that the best things are kept for crate time.

- If you are leaving your puppy on their own in their crate for any length of time when you are not around, always remember to please take off their collar, as it can be a safety issue.

- Leave the door open to the crate during the day, so your puppy can come and go as he chooses.

- You can leave his bed in his crate during the day, as well as during the night. He will naturally go into the crate to rest and relax, as that is where his bed is.

- Your puppy should want to go in on his own (when he is tired during the day and at night for bedtime) or when he needs a break from visitors or children.

- You can try a bit of training and say, "Into Bed" while pointing into his bed in the crate and throwing some of his favorite treats into his bed, in his crate. Consider putting his favorite toy in and his favorite blanket too..

- Please note that puppy should Not be approached when he is in his crate (people should not put hands into the crate to pet him). This will make him feel safe and secure and he will understand that the crate is his safe place and he will want to go in voluntarily!

- Remember, use the crate to reinforce your Daily Routine with your puppy (eating-drinking /toileting/sleeping).

Toilet Training Tips

- Patience and consistency are key throughout this process. Hang in there. Pretty much every dog can be toilet trained! Don't worry!

- Remember to reward/praise when your puppy gets it right. He will be very keen to please you, so positive reinforcement is important.

- If you use a crate from the start you will greatly reduce the time it takes to fully toilet train your dog. Dogs are very reluctant to soil where they sleep so they learn to hold it.

- Most puppies can sleep 7 hours without needing to go to the toilet. So, during the day and first thing after you wake up in the morning, aim to help your puppy get to where you want him to toilet, as soon as pos-sible.

- Monitoring puppy behavior very closely will speed up the toilet train-ing process.

- Key times for toileting are:

  o When your puppy wakes up after sleeping (so after naps during the day as well as the night-time sleep).
  o After meals.
  o After drinks.
  o After play / excitement.

- How do you tell if your puppy needs the toilet?
  Your puppy will start to circle/sniff/crouch. As soon as you see this, you must move quickly outdoors, encouraging your puppy to follow you. Always bring him to the same spot, as his scent will encourage him to go.

- When your puppy toilets...give lots of praise!

Week 1 Potty Training Tracker

Day	Time			Notes
Day 1		Poop	Pee	
		Poop	Pee	
		Poop	Pee	
		Poop	Pee	
		Poop	Pee	
		Poop	Pee	
		Poop	Pee	
Day 2		Poop	Pee	
		Poop	Pee	
		Poop	Pee	
		Poop	Pee	
		Poop	Pee	
		Poop	Pee	
		Poop	Pee	
Day 3		Poop	Pee	
		Poop	Pee	
		Poop	Pee	
		Poop	Pee	
		Poop	Pee	
		Poop	Pee	
		Poop	Pee	
Day 4		Poop	Pee	
		Poop	Pee	
		Poop	Pee	
		Poop	Pee	
		Poop	Pee	
		Poop	Pee	
		Poop	Pee	
Day 5		Poop	Pee	
		Poop	Pee	
		Poop	Pee	
		Poop	Pee	
		Poop	Pee	
		Poop	Pee	
		Poop	Pee	
Day 6		Poop	Pee	
		Poop	Pee	
		Poop	Pee	
		Poop	Pee	
		Poop	Pee	
		Poop	Pee	
		Poop	Pee	
Day 7		Poop	Pee	
		Poop	Pee	
		Poop	Pee	
		Poop	Pee	
		Poop	Pee	
		Poop	Pee	

Week 2   🌀 Potty Training Tracker

Day	Time			Notes
Day 1		Poop	Pee	
		Poop	Pee	
		Poop	Pee	
		Poop	Pee	
		Poop	Pee	
		Poop	Pee	
		Poop	Pee	
Day 2		Poop	Pee	
		Poop	Pee	
		Poop	Pee	
		Poop	Pee	
		Poop	Pee	
		Poop	Pee	
		Poop	Pee	
Day 3		Poop	Pee	
		Poop	Pee	
		Poop	Pee	
		Poop	Pee	
		Poop	Pee	
		Poop	Pee	
		Poop	Pee	
Day 4		Poop	Pee	
		Poop	Pee	
		Poop	Pee	
		Poop	Pee	
		Poop	Pee	
		Poop	Pee	
		Poop	Pee	
Day 5		Poop	Pee	
		Poop	Pee	
		Poop	Pee	
		Poop	Pee	
		Poop	Pee	
		Poop	Pee	
		Poop	Pee	
Day 6		Poop	Pee	
		Poop	Pee	
		Poop	Pee	
		Poop	Pee	
		Poop	Pee	
		Poop	Pee	
		Poop	Pee	
Day 7		Poop	Pee	
		Poop	Pee	
		Poop	Pee	
		Poop	Pee	
		Poop	Pee	
		Poop	Pee	

Week 3

Potty Training Tracker

Day	Time			Notes
Day 1		Poop	Pee	
		Poop	Pee	
		Poop	Pee	
		Poop	Pee	
		Poop	Pee	
		Poop	Pee	
		Poop	Pee	
Day 2		Poop	Pee	
		Poop	Pee	
		Poop	Pee	
		Poop	Pee	
		Poop	Pee	
		Poop	Pee	
		Poop	Pee	
Day 3		Poop	Pee	
		Poop	Pee	
		Poop	Pee	
		Poop	Pee	
		Poop	Pee	
		Poop	Pee	
		Poop	Pee	
Day 4		Poop	Pee	
		Poop	Pee	
		Poop	Pee	
		Poop	Pee	
		Poop	Pee	
		Poop	Pee	
		Poop	Pee	
Day 5		Poop	Pee	
		Poop	Pee	
		Poop	Pee	
		Poop	Pee	
		Poop	Pee	
		Poop	Pee	
		Poop	Pee	
Day 6		Poop	Pee	
		Poop	Pee	
		Poop	Pee	
		Poop	Pee	
		Poop	Pee	
		Poop	Pee	
		Poop	Pee	
Day 7		Poop	Pee	
		Poop	Pee	
		Poop	Pee	
		Poop	Pee	
		Poop	Pee	
		Poop	Pee	
		Poop	Pee	

Week 4 💩 Potty Training Tracker

Day	Time			Notes
		Poop	Pee	
		Poop	Pee	
		Poop	Pee	
Day 1		Poop	Pee	
		Poop	Pee	
		Poop	Pee	
		Poop	Pee	
		Poop	Pee	
		Poop	Pee	
		Poop	Pee	
Day 2		Poop	Pee	
		Poop	Pee	
		Poop	Pee	
		Poop	Pee	
		Poop	Pee	
		Poop	Pee	
		Poop	Pee	
Day 3		Poop	Pee	
		Poop	Pee	
		Poop	Pee	
		Poop	Pee	
		Poop	Pee	
		Poop	Pee	
		Poop	Pee	
Day 4		Poop	Pee	
		Poop	Pee	
		Poop	Pee	
		Poop	Pee	
		Poop	Pee	
		Poop	Pee	
		Poop	Pee	
Day 5		Poop	Pee	
		Poop	Pee	
		Poop	Pee	
		Poop	Pee	
		Poop	Pee	
		Poop	Pee	
		Poop	Pee	
Day 6		Poop	Pee	
		Poop	Pee	
		Poop	Pee	
		Poop	Pee	
		Poop	Pee	
		Poop	Pee	
		Poop	Pee	
Day 7		Poop	Pee	
		Poop	Pee	
		Poop	Pee	
		Poop	Pee	

Ode to Man's Best Friend

My dog lives in the moment
She's as happy as can be
She does not worry, cry or frown
And gives her love for free

Always a good attitude
Living each day to the full
She runs and naps and walks and plays
Her favorite game is "Pull"

When I'm sad and lonely
She puts her head upon my lap
Those big brown eyes look up at me
And say, cheer up old chap

My dog lives in the moment
A lesson for us all
Loving, loyal and wonderful
And will even fetch the ball!

Fiona Gamble, 2020

My Canine Friends

Dog friends I like to play with:

Name   Breed

_____   _____

_____   _____

My Favorite: _____

_____

What I like to do with them: _____

_____

_____

Adventures we have had: _____

_____

_____

_____

Golden Retriever
Things you should know...

- While there are certainly exceptions, as a general rule, Golden retrievers are not watchdogs. They love everyone! They are always up for a belly rub no matter who.

- If you have a beautiful landscaped garden, expect some damage. Golden retrievers love digging! They also love mud, so in addition to digging, Golden retrievers also tend to play, sleep, or roll in flower beds!

- Goldens are unaware of their size can make for some funny moments when they want in on the action in a family hug. They would be happy also to hop of your lap if you let them!

- Unfortunately, Golden retrievers are prone to waxy ears. This tends to be a result of poor air circulation due to their long ears. Keep their ears clean and dry as much as possible and make sure to have a look inside regularly to make sure no excess wax is build-ing up.

- Twice a year, once in the fall and once in the spring, Golden retrievers will experience their most heavy shedding. Light-mod-erate shedding occurs all year. With a Golden in the house, you will always have dog fur around, even with regular dusting and vacu-uming. You may even find that when you replace furnishings or floors you will look to match it with your pet's fur color.

- Golden Retrievers have a tendency to follow their nose, so for their own safety, they should not be allowed to roam freely.

- Goldens are enthusiastic family members. As a family pet, especially with children, the breed has few equals, but Golden Retrievers are more than just a family pet, they are loyal best friends and loving family members. They can sometime seem needy and are usually to be found at your feet. Watch out! They are a tripping hazard!

- Golden Retrievers love food. Unfortunately, the breed has a tendency to overeat, and because of this, they can easily become overweight or even obese.

- There are exceptions, but generally speaking, Golden Retrievers have a natural love for water so be extra careful not to leave them loose near water if you do not want them to go in. On posi-tive note, they are a joy to take to take to the beach.

- Being intelligent, they needs mental as well as physical stimula-tion. Be sure to play with them lot and have some different toys for them to play with when they are home alone. Warning! Bored Goldens get up to all sorts of Mischief!

Feeding Your Dog

- How best to feed your dog depends on the breed and size of your dog. Your vet and many on line reputable guides and books will give you specific guidelines.

- Remember that puppies need to eat more regularly and have different nutritional needs so over time you will need to adapt their diet accordingly.

- You should keep a record of the food they are eating, how often and how much. This may help if they get a stomach upset as you will be able to identify anything unusual they may have had. When dogs have an upset stomach they usuallly get diarrhoea or will vomit.

- Most vets will recommend a dried food that that provides for all nutritional needs for your puppy. There so many varieties avail-able in pet shops now. Dogs should be given that same food all the time and you should not vary or / change it from one day to the next.

- If you are advised to change your puppy's food, do it gradually mixing the regular with the new over the course of a week or so increasing the amount of new food each day until their meal is made up of 100% new.

- Always make sure to have water freely available to your dog at all times. It helps to have a large bowl so it will will last a while betwen refills.

- Try and keep treats to a minimum. While you are training your dog consider holding some of their meal back and using it as a reward instead of giving them extra.

 # Food Record

As your puppy grows you will need to adapt the food and amounts given.

Food	Age	Amount per day	Notes

Favorite Treats _____

_____

Food Sensitivities

A food sensitivity is a reaction to ingredients in food that your dog's body does not tolerate well. This is very common. Food sensitivities are an individual issue and every dog is different. If your dog has diarrhoea regularly or vomits especially just after eating, he may have food sensitivities. Talk to your vet. They may recommend trying a new food. Keep track of any food you believe your pooch may be sensitive to.

Food	Date	Reaction / Notes

General Training Tips

- Start in a quiet environment that has few distractions. Pick a time when your puppy is not too tired and possibly a little hungry. Always have fun. Never train your dog when you are in bad mood.

- Wait until your pup does something good. Now reward with a treat.

- When asking a dog to do a behavior like sit, make sure you help the dog into the sit position after the command has been given. When helping a dog to learn sit just place the treat above his nose and lure back just enough that he sits. Now treat and praise.

- Each time you go into a new environment or pick training up on a new day it is like starting all over again. So take it slow and you may have to go back to helping your dog.

- Play with your dog. This creates a wonderful bond and tells the dog it is fun to work and be near you. Be light hearted. Smile and laugh at your dog. They love to make us laugh!

- Praise your dog enthusiastically when they have done some thing right. Dogs sometimes even seem to like it if you clap for them.

- You can also use their food as the treat. Having your dog work for each meal is very rewarding. Most dogs love to work one piece of food at a time. Dogs love praise and treats while working, some dogs even love a pat on the chest.

- Over the next few pages you will find the top 6 behaviors every dog should learn. Be sure to focus on these first before you get to the fun stuff. There are lots of resources to help you on line also including lots of videos to show how it is done.

Training Skill Sit

Sit is a good one to teach first because it's natural concept for most dogs. It's therefore also one of the easiest for them to learn, so even pets who are new to training can get the hang of it within a few sessions. And because it's also a transition command, once a dog can sit, you can move on to other commands

Date	Repetition (tick or circle)	Progress Notes
	🐾 🐾 🐾 🐾 🐾	
	🐾 🐾 🐾 🐾 🐾	
	🐾 🐾 🐾 🐾 🐾	
	🐾 🐾 🐾 🐾 🐾	
	🐾 🐾 🐾 🐾 🐾	
	🐾 🐾 🐾 🐾 🐾	
	🐾 🐾 🐾 🐾 🐾	
	🐾 🐾 🐾 🐾 🐾	
	🐾 🐾 🐾 🐾 🐾	
	🐾 🐾 🐾 🐾 🐾	

Achieved   Date:_____

Training Skill DOWN/LAY DOWN

A standing dog could easily bolt in a flash because there's nothing keeping her in place. A sitting dog is like a car in Park, but it's still easy for her to get on out of there. But when she's lying down, it's like she is on pause or hold. Because the command helps you control your dog, it's also a great transition to more complicated tricks like rolling over or playing dead.

Date	Repetition (tick or circle)	Progress Notes

Achieved   Date:_____

31

Training Skill
Stay

This is one of the most important skills for any dog to learn as a dog who knows how to stay won't run into the street if she gets loose, so. This one is best to teach when your pup is tired and hungry so she won't get too hyper to focus. And be patient: Most dogs take at least a few of days to understand Stay and it can take a few weeks to master it. But because it protects your dog from danger, keep a bag of treats handy and keep practicing until she's a pro.

Date	Repetition (tick or circle)	Progress Notes

Achieved   Date:_____

Training Skill

COME

If you plan to take your dog anywhere off-leash, she must know how to come when called. It can keep her safe at the dog park if a fight breaks out, get her away from the danger if she breaks off the leash, or ensures she stays close when walking in the woods or just fooling around in the backyard. It a good idea to teach Stay first as this is a good point from where to issue the request to Come.

Date	Repetition (tick or circle)	Progress Notes

Achieved   Date:_____

Training Skill

HEEL

Dogs of all sizes should learn to heel, or walk calmly by your side, especially if you exercise your pup in busy town areas where there's not much room on the sidewalk. The skill is even more important for large or strong pups who naturally pull on the leash. Once a dog can heel, walks will be easier and more pleasant for your dog and you.

Date	Repetition (tick or circle)	Progress Notes
	🐾🐾🐾🐾🐾🐾🐾🐾🐾🐾	
	🐾🐾🐾🐾🐾🐾🐾🐾🐾🐾	
	🐾🐾🐾🐾🐾🐾🐾🐾🐾🐾	
	🐾🐾🐾🐾🐾🐾🐾🐾🐾🐾	
	🐾🐾🐾🐾🐾🐾🐾🐾🐾🐾	
	🐾🐾🐾🐾🐾🐾🐾🐾🐾🐾	
	🐾🐾🐾🐾🐾🐾🐾🐾🐾🐾	
	🐾🐾🐾🐾🐾🐾🐾🐾🐾🐾	
	🐾🐾🐾🐾🐾🐾🐾🐾🐾🐾	
	🐾🐾🐾🐾🐾🐾🐾🐾🐾🐾	

Achieved   Date:_____

34

Training Skill

No

No covers multiple situations like when you pup goes to investigate a discarded coffee cup on the street or when you want them to stop doing something like jumping up on a person. No makes a good, all-purpose command for everything you want your pup NOT to do.

Date	Repetition (tick or circle)	Progress Notes

Achieved   Date:_____

Training Skill _____

Description, Goal:

_____

_____

_____

Date	Repetition (tick or circle)	Progress Notes
	🐾 🐾 🐾 🐾 🐾 🐾 🐾 🐾 🐾 🐾	
	🐾 🐾 🐾 🐾 🐾 🐾 🐾 🐾 🐾 🐾	
	🐾 🐾 🐾 🐾 🐾 🐾 🐾 🐾 🐾 🐾	
	🐾 🐾 🐾 🐾 🐾 🐾 🐾 🐾 🐾 🐾	
	🐾 🐾 🐾 🐾 🐾 🐾 🐾 🐾 🐾 🐾	
	🐾 🐾 🐾 🐾 🐾 🐾 🐾 🐾 🐾 🐾	
	🐾 🐾 🐾 🐾 🐾 🐾 🐾 🐾 🐾 🐾	
	🐾 🐾 🐾 🐾 🐾 🐾 🐾 🐾 🐾 🐾	
	🐾 🐾 🐾 🐾 🐾 🐾 🐾 🐾 🐾	
	🐾 🐾 🐾 🐾 🐾 🐾 🐾 🐾 🐾	

Achieved   Date: _____

36

Training Skill _____

Description, Goal:

_____

_____

_____

Date	Repetition (tick or circle)	Progress Notes

 Achieved   Date:_____

37

Training Skill

_____

Description, Goal:

_____

_____

_____

Date	Repetition (tick or circle)	Progress Notes
	🐾 🐾 🐾 🐾 🐾 🐾 🐾 🐾 🐾 🐾	
	🐾 🐾 🐾 🐾 🐾 🐾 🐾 🐾 🐾 🐾	
	🐾 🐾 🐾 🐾 🐾 🐾 🐾 🐾 🐾 🐾	
	🐾 🐾 🐾 🐾 🐾 🐾 🐾 🐾 🐾 🐾	
	🐾 🐾 🐾 🐾 🐾 🐾 🐾 🐾 🐾 🐾	
	🐾 🐾 🐾 🐾 🐾 🐾 🐾 🐾 🐾 🐾	
	🐾 🐾 🐾 🐾 🐾 🐾 🐾 🐾 🐾 🐾	
	🐾 🐾 🐾 🐾 🐾 🐾 🐾 🐾 🐾 🐾	
	🐾 🐾 🐾 🐾 🐾 🐾 🐾 🐾 🐾 🐾	
	🐾 🐾 🐾 🐾 🐾 🐾 🐾 🐾 🐾 🐾	

Achieved   Date:_____

Training Skill _____

Description, Goal:

_____

_____

_____

Date	Repetition (tick or circle)	Progress Notes
	🐾🐾 🐾🐾 🐾🐾 🐾🐾 🐾🐾 🐾 🐾 🐾 🐾	
	🐾🐾 🐾🐾 🐾🐾 🐾🐾 🐾🐾 🐾 🐾 🐾 🐾	
	🐾🐾 🐾🐾 🐾🐾 🐾🐾 🐾🐾 🐾 🐾 🐾 🐾	
	🐾🐾 🐾🐾 🐾🐾 🐾🐾 🐾🐾 🐾 🐾 🐾 🐾	
	🐾🐾 🐾🐾 🐾🐾 🐾🐾 🐾🐾 🐾 🐾 🐾	
	🐾🐾 🐾🐾 🐾🐾 🐾🐾 🐾🐾 🐾 🐾 🐾	
	🐾🐾 🐾🐾 🐾🐾 🐾🐾 🐾🐾 🐾 🐾 🐾	
	🐾🐾 🐾🐾 🐾🐾 🐾🐾 🐾🐾 🐾 🐾 🐾	
	🐾🐾 🐾🐾 🐾🐾 🐾🐾 🐾🐾	
	🐾🐾 🐾🐾 🐾🐾 🐾🐾 🐾🐾 🐾 🐾 🐾	

Achieved   Date:_____

Training Skill

_____

Description, Goal:

_____

_____

_____

Date	Repetition (tick or circle)	Progress Notes
	🐾 🐾 🐾 🐾 🐾 🐾 🐾 🐾 🐾	
	🐾 🐾 🐾 🐾 🐾 🐾 🐾 🐾 🐾	
	🐾 🐾 🐾 🐾 🐾 🐾 🐾 🐾 🐾	
	🐾 🐾 🐾 🐾 🐾 🐾 🐾 🐾 🐾	
	🐾 🐾 🐾 🐾 🐾 🐾 🐾 🐾 🐾	
	🐾 🐾 🐾 🐾 🐾 🐾 🐾 🐾 🐾	
	🐾 🐾 🐾 🐾 🐾 🐾 🐾 🐾 🐾	
	🐾 🐾 🐾 🐾 🐾 🐾 🐾 🐾 🐾	
	🐾 🐾 🐾 🐾 🐾 🐾 🐾 🐾 🐾	
	🐾 🐾 🐾 🐾 🐾 🐾 🐾 🐾 🐾	

Achieved   Date:_____

Training Skill _____

Description, Goal:

_____

_____

_____

Date	Repetition (tick or circle)	Progress Notes
	🐾🐾🐾🐾🐾 🐾🐾🐾🐾	
	🐾🐾🐾🐾🐾 🐾🐾🐾🐾	
	🐾🐾🐾🐾🐾 🐾🐾🐾🐾	
	🐾🐾🐾🐾🐾 🐾🐾🐾🐾	
	🐾🐾🐾🐾🐾 🐾🐾🐾🐾	
	🐾🐾🐾🐾🐾 🐾🐾🐾🐾	
	🐾🐾🐾🐾🐾 🐾🐾🐾🐾	
	🐾🐾🐾🐾🐾 🐾🐾🐾🐾	
	🐾🐾🐾🐾🐾 🐾🐾🐾🐾	
	🐾🐾🐾🐾🐾 🐾🐾🐾🐾	

Achieved   Date:_____

Puppy Socialization

• To ensure that your puppy grows into a happy, calm dog with no behavioral issues you will need to expose him to as many varied experiences as possible. This includes other animals and people outside the home as well a range of events, environments and situations. This process is called socialization.

• Experiences during the first year of a dog's life can make a world of difference to their future temperament and character. If you take the time to socialise your puppy you have the best chance of friendly, well-adjusted adult dog who enjoys the company of people, can be taken anywhere and lives life to the max!

• A puppy who lacks experience of the world will find many things that we take for granted frightening and is very likely to grow up to be a nervous dog. A frightened and anxious dog is more likely to develop behaviour problems than a dog who has had a rich, varied and positive puppyhood.

• Over the next few pages you can keep track of all the key things that you need to expose your puppy to. Depending on where you live and the household you live you you can add in in your own too.

The sooner you start socialization the better!

Socialization Check List
Contact with People

	✓	✓	✓	✓	✓	Notes
Holding puppy						
Touching paws						
Touching muzzle						
Touching Ears						
Touching Tail						
Hugging puppy						
Checking teeth						
Clipping nails						
Brushing teeth						
Checking between pads						
Cleaning ears						
Touching rear legs						
Tickling belly						
Brushing / Grooming						

Socialization Check List
Interacting with People

		✓	✓	✓	✓	Notes
Men with	Beards					
	Hat					
	Sunglasses					
	Jewelry					
	Helmets					
	Cigarettes					
Women with	Hat					
	Sunglasses					
	Jewelry					
	Helmets					
	Cigarettes					
Children	0-2					
	In strollers					
	2-4 yrs					
	4-12 yrs					
	13-19 yrs					
Adults with	Crutches					
	Canes					
	Wheel chairs					
Elderly person	Male					
	Female					
People	Shouting					
	Laughing					
	Crying					
	Arguing					
	Playing					

_____

_____

_____

_____

Socialization Check List
Visual and Noise

	✓	Date	Notes
Sirens			
Fireworks			
Car Horns			
Traffic			
Thunderstorms			
Shopping Malls			
Crowds of people			
Airplanes			
Helicopters			
Wheelchairs			
Crutches/ Canes			
Bicycles			
Skateboards			
Radios			
Loud Cars			
Motorbikes			
Parking Lots			
Doorbells			
Trucks			
Trains			

Socialization Check List
Meeting Other Animals

	✓	✓	✓	✓	✓	Notes
Puppies						
Male adult dogs						
Female adult dogs						
Kittens						
Cats						
Horses						
Cow						
Sheep						
Chickens						
Ducks						
Birds						

Notes

_____

_____

_____

_____

_____

_____

Memorable Adventure

Date _____

Where _____

_____

With _____

Memorable Adventure

Date _____

Where _____

_____

With _____

Memorable Adventure

Date _____

Where _____

_____

With _____

Memorable Adventure

Date _____

Where _____

_____

With _____

If you have any pictures you can stick them here

Memorable Adventure

Date _____

Where _____

_____

With _____

My First Christmas

Stick a picture here!

My First Birthday

Stick a picture here!

Grooming

Just as your own personal hygiene is essential, pet grooming is essential for your pet's overall health and well being.   Done regularly, pet grooming keeps the coat of your four legged friend in tip top shape. It also provides an opportunity to make sure your pet is free from nasty pests like fleas and ticks as well as getting up close and personal to check your pets skin and ears for signs of any problems.

Grooming includes a number of different activities including brushing, bathing, cutting, ear and eye care. See below a guideline for the frequency recommended for each of these activities.

Nail Clipping	Brushing	Teeth Brushing
once a month	once a week	twice a week
Bath	**Ears, eyes and paws**	**Hair Trimming**
every 2 weeks	every 2 weeks	once a month

- Brushing:
  Use a special high quality brush good for your dogs type of hair. Brushing helps to remove tangles and mats and makes his hair shiny and healthy. It will also help to remove any debris from the outdoors. Consult with your vet or pet store on the best type of brush for your dog.

- Bathing:
  When bathing your pet, fill a tub with warm water (not hot). Regular soap will not be good for your pet's skin so you will need to find a good pet shampoo at your local pet supply shop. Lather up using a small amount of shampoo and rinse well. Ideally you also blow dry your pet for a complete finish.

- Paw care:
  Your pooch may not like you at their paws so much but it is important to check for any matted hair around the paws and to make sure they are generally clean to avoid any nasty infections. You should also trim the fur to level it with the foot and clip the hook of the nail. Using a dog nail clippers, ensure to only trim the very end dead bit of the nail and not the live part.

- Ear and eye care:
  Regularly clean both eyes and ears. You can use warm salty water with cotton wool to clean around the eyes. A cotton bud can be used to very gently clean the ears. You should only clean the part of the ear you can see and don't ever stick anything right into it.

- Dental Hygiene:
  It is best to teach your dog to accept tooth brushing while he is still a puppy. In order to be successful at brushing your dog's teeth, you must make it a positive and fun experience for both of you. Praise your pooch throughout the whole procedure, with reassurance through every step. For best results, start out brushing his teeth with your finger. Gradually progress to using some toothpaste with your finger and finally introduce a brush after a few days.

- You can do all the steps listed above yourself, however professional dog groomers really do an amazing job so consider once in a while booking your pooch in for a mini spa day. It is also a great opportunity for your dog to socialize and have some fun. It is expensive though and not every dog likes it.

Grooming Log

Date	Time	Treatment	Notes	Cost
		Bath ☐ Brush ☐ Dematting ☐ Nails ☐ Cut ☐ Ears ☐ Teeth ☐		
		Bath ☐ Brush ☐ Dematting ☐ Nails ☐ Cut ☐ Ears ☐ Teeth ☐		
		Bath ☐ Brush ☐ Dematting ☐ Nails ☐ Cut ☐ Ears ☐ Teeth ☐		
		Bath ☐ Brush ☐ Dematting ☐ Nails ☐ Cut ☐ Ears ☐ Teeth ☐		
		Bath ☐ Brush ☐ Dematting ☐ Nails ☐ Cut ☐ Ears ☐ Teeth ☐		
		Bath ☐ Brush ☐ Dematting ☐ Nails ☐ Cut ☐ Ears ☐ Teeth ☐		
		Bath ☐ Brush ☐ Dematting ☐ Nails ☐ Cut ☐ Ears ☐ Teeth ☐		
		Bath ☐ Brush ☐ Dematting ☐ Nails ☐ Cut ☐ Ears ☐ Teeth ☐		
		Bath ☐ Brush ☐ Dematting ☐ Nails ☐ Cut ☐ Ears ☐ Teeth ☐		

Groomer details : _____

_____

Health Records

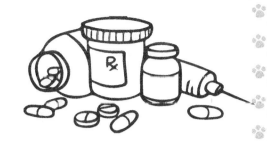

Description	Date	Treatment	Notes

Flea, Tick
& Wormer Tracker

Month		Date
	Flea /Tick	
	Wormer	
	Flea /Tick	
	Wormer	
	Flea /Tick	
	Wormer	
	Flea /Tick	
	Wormer	
	Flea /Tick	
	Wormer	
	Flea /Tick	
	Wormer	
	Flea /Tick	
	Wormer	
	Flea /Tick	
	Wormer	
	Flea /Tick	
	Wormer	
	Flea /Tick	
	Wormer	
	Flea /Tick	
	Wormer	
	Flea /Tick	
	Wormer	

Weight Tracker

It is important to keep an eye on your pupp␣s weight to ensure they are in the right weight range for their age and breed.

Weight	Date	Age	Notes

Walkies!

Keep track of your dailly walks here:

Date	Location	Mins	Notes

Walkies!

Keep track of your daily walks here:

Date	Location	Mins	Notes

Walkies!

Keep track of your daily walks here:

Date	Location	Mins	Notes

Walkies!

Keep track of your daily walks here:

Date	Location	Mins	Notes

Walkies!

Keep track of your dailly walks here:

Date	Location	Mins	Notes

Walkies!

Keep track of your daily walks here:

Date	Location	Mins	Notes

Memories/ Notes/ Pics

Memories/ Notes/ Pics

Memories/ Notes/ Pics

Memories/ Notes/ Pics

Memories/ Notes/ Pics

_____

_____

_____

_____

_____

_____

_____

_____

_____

_____

_____

_____

_____

_____

_____

_____

Memories/ Notes/ Pics

_____
_____
_____
_____
_____
_____
_____
_____
_____
_____
_____
_____
_____
_____
_____
_____
_____

Memories/ Notes/ Pics

_____

_____

_____

_____

_____

_____

_____

_____

_____

_____

_____

_____

_____

_____

_____

_____

_____

Memories/ Notes/ Pics

_____
_____
_____
_____
_____
_____
_____
_____
_____
_____
_____
_____
_____
_____
_____
_____
_____

Memories/ Notes/ Pics

Memories/ Notes/ Pics

_____

_____

_____

_____

_____

_____

_____

_____

_____

_____

_____

_____

_____

_____

_____

_____

_____

_____

Useful Contacts

Groomer, Pet Store, Dog Walker, Doggy Day care

Name: _____

Address: _____

Phone number: _____

Opening hours: _____

Name: _____

Address: _____

Phone number: _____

Opening hours: _____

Name: _____

Address: _____

Phone number: _____

Opening hours: _____

Name: _____

Address: _____

Phone number: _____

Opening hours: _____

Printed in Great Britain
by Amazon

39736030R00046